NOTHING OF THE MONTH CLUB

Alessandrelli

All rights reserved; no part of this book may be reproduced by any means without the publisher's permission.

ISBN:978-1-913642-50-1

The author/s has asserted their right to be identified as the author of this Work in accordance with the Copyright, Designs and Patents Act 1988

Book designed by Aaron Kent

Edited by Aaron Kent

Broken Sleep Books (2021), Talgarreg, Wales

Contents

"The problem of America is my body."	7
The Leopard Does Not Change Its Spots	**11**
Everyday Dilemma	**19**
The Annunciation	20
The Third Sitting Room	21
Your X-Rays Have Just Come Back from the Lab and We Think We Know What Your Problem Is	23
Nothing of the Month Club	**25**
Nothing of the Month Club	26
Nothing of the Month Club	27
Nothing of the Month Club	28
Nothing of the Month Club	29
Nothing of the Month Club	30
Nothing of the Month Club	31
Nothing of the Month Club	32
Nothing of the Month Club	33
Nothing of the Month Club	34
Nothing of the Month Club	35
Nothing of the Month Club	36
Nothing of the Month Club	37
Nothing of the Month Club	38
Resignation Modes	**41**
The Natural Way To Draw	**55**
The Puppy Still Hasn't Opened Her Eyes	56
Monkey Puzzle Roots	57
Last Exit	58
Stray	61
Notes	65
Acknowledgements	67

Nothing of the Month Club

Jeff Alessandrelli

"The problem of America is my body."
after Alice Notley

Every gustatory pleasure
is a field
that will one day fail
to provide pasture.
Or
I'm worried
about my belly fat again,
home alone every night,
dusting,
doing dishes,
my 34th winter.
Noisier the leaves
seem to get
the deeper into November
one goes,
muddier the sun.
Suddenly under-
dreaming
my days away,
all worthwhile interests
waning,
my favorite book
merely
the girl with the best ass
in the neighborhood,
the only poem
that tempts me
her boyfriend
working out in his apartment
in the gloaming's half-light,
his phosphorescent 6 pack abs.
Insomnia's eternity,
glutton for drudgery,
hours later I'm up
before dawn,
thinking about the sign

outside my favorite taqueria
that reads
No Shirt, No Shoes, No Problem;
the way the shards of afternoon
sun seem
to make it glow
neon-bright.
There I sit at my corner table for hours,
ignoring the herds of cars and buses
that pass by and pass on.
Outside this fiefdom
the problem of America
is my body
but inside I am swallowing
so many different poisons
at such breakneck speed
as to actualize myself
invincible.
So it matters little
how important my mouth is
to my throat, my lips
to my gums, the charbroil-seared
sound of my voice
to my belly's girth.
Walking home at dark,
noisier the leaves seem to get
with each step.
And pockmarked and pristine,
looming larger and larger,
the moon.

The Leopard Does Not Change Its Spots
"Any awkward moment is a creative act."
--Ai Weiwei

THE INVENTION OF SOLITUDE BEGINS IN CHILDHOOD

An only child, I grew up with what seemed like two impenetrable adults looming overhead, one continually sawing the air with his hands like a crazed orchestra conductor, the other whispering to me in calm, measured tones that seemed to only solidify my unknowing. The socialized decency that makes effective communication impossible for so many people was engrained in me at a very young age—when I cried I was held and shushed into a caress, but when I laughed or pointed a haze of silence was etched in the air. By the age of 5 I was proficient at being silent in English and Spanish. By 10 I was an expert in silence in 13 different languages, among them Muskum, Chehalis and Burgundian. However and whenever I spoke, I spoke in a way that announced a futuring both far distant and as near as sky to blue. I was the type of child that always wanted something more from a sunset, one that worked too hard at being himself. The anxious kind, with bones made of 24 karat gold and flexilight plastic, possessor of a smile that even in its fullness seemed to glint with nervous apprehension.

Ants, Near and Out of Sight

As I grew older I sent mail, postal mail. This was the pre internet era, mid to late 1990s, a period when everything was on the cusp of rampant digitality but for most folks in America the internet was still a CD-ROM sent unbidden from AOL, one promising 50 or 100 free hours of the world wide web for 45 or 60 days. (Payment was a carpenter ant, forever seen in the distance but too incessantly small to squash.) These compact discs arrived constantly at my parents' house but being that we didn't get a family computer until I was a senior in high school postal mail had to suffice. I miss this disconnection now. Home alone after school, restless, someone's shadow was always working like a hammer behind me as I stuffed envelopes and carefully positioned stamps. No one was ever there.

Too Easy to Make Work

First encountering most of them through an open solicitation call in the back pages of *Highlights* magazine, I had 14 pen pals: 11 in the U.S., 1 in Canada, 1 in England, 1 in Thailand. Who and where they were mattered less to me, though, than what I sent and received back from them. Most of my pals were purely pleasantries, our three-to-four times a year exchanges a combination of misguided sociality and the earnest desire for friendship. Porous, our relationship exacerbated by the burden of geography's long grasps, these friends soon proved to be strangers to me, our correspondence faltering soon after it had begun.

"I Lost my Virginity to a Rainbow."

Older than me by what seemed to be a beguiling amount of years, my pen pal from England fancied himself a visionary of sorts, sending letters that began "Last week I lost my virginity to a rainbow skying above Trinity College in Dublin, the heavens desiccating their eternal glories for treasures that only lie beneath." Lasting just two exchanges, our correspondence ended when my mother read the above and, her eyes housing small fires, two dull blue flames, angrily called my father at work.

An Oasis of Grids and Centaurs

Although for years we regularly exchanged expressive drawings and Venn diagrams, each a deep state conspiracy against the primacy of language, eventually my pen pal from Thailand's replies slowed to a crawl, then a stop. Sent 14 months after I'd last written him, his final missive to me contained the only sentence in English he'd ever included in a letter: *Yesterday I woke from a bad apple and now I turn around my back.*

A Mammal's Half Life Lasts Still Longer

You get older, are older, use words like *granular*, *aphasic* and *lack*. When someone writes the sentence "The wisdom possessed by the elderly is only gained because they cannot remember (or forgive) the passion they once so dearly prized" you understand it in a way that you previously thought impossible. All of the things that were once more important to you than everything else now matter less and less; an aging dog grown tired of chasing its tail. Concerto finished, one of your parents is dead; the other speaks little, aggressively little, in a voice as soft as the humanless snow of a ghost. Silence. Knowing what they're made of, as you age you excavate your bones flake by flake, boil the residue for the cash the scrap brings. Purely for the joy of the world you used to send your pen pals freshly formed icicles, green and red water balloons filled with lemonade, a papier-mâché cat with comically oversized paws and a rabid sunspot for a tongue. Now the very phrase "pen pal" seems absurd to you. All this and yet still your whole life still seems to revolve around and live within the moment when you were 15 years old and opened a letter from a new pen pal that, in a mannered and calculated calligraphy, light blue ink, simply had the words *PLEASE BE WITH ME* written up and down, over and over, on two 8.25 x 11 sheets of pristine white paper. You hid the letter from your parents, tried to search the sender's identity, attempted to calculate a response. But with too much and not enough to say, you never responded. *PLEASE BE WITH ME.* Most days now you drive through town, work a job, listen to music, have dinner with friends. *PLEASE.* There's half a life there. *BE WITH ME.* I close my eyes more than I think these days. Even nonexistent insects annoy me. Graduate of the School of the Furtive Movement and Roiled Fetter, in the dark I close my eyes. Please.

Everyday Dilemma

This breath took me all the previous breaths to reach it. I'm barely keeping up, constantly worried that I might have missed a breath somewhere distant in time's past. But if I come upon that breath now, unsated, what to do? To breathe it would cause me to lose the breath that I would have breathed had I not been breathing that one lost long ago, thus occasioning me to, again, lose my breath, this present breath I'm currently breathing. In finding one breath I would lose another again, ad infinitum. What a dilemma! In searching, I fear to find myself whole, broken; in neglecting to search, I fear losing the splinters of what I might have once become. Deep within myself, I draw the shades of my apartment and concentrate, some studied monotone of hope and bone.

The Annunciation

With her bowel movement my three-year old daughter beheads God, clean, precise. I admire the smell as though it were a piece of dirty jewelry spotted amidst flurries of falling snow. Feeble, my lack's fortitude mottled with crow's feet, I smile at the other passengers on the bus. Against the bouncing fluorescence some limpid waste of a moon out the shifting windows covers no one fully except my daughter, her hands absently explaining to her mouth the parameters of sensation. Already she is a slave to her life. Waft—it's an answer to a question no one's asked, right? A problem of proximity and degree? What does—she wafts in it. Later I stare at the body, head boundless and sinewed. Pacing without moving, my daughter sits in my lap.

The Third Sitting Room

For years I dreamed of writing a novel about napkins. Although the book would encompass other themes and topics, from competitive archery to one hapless dreamer's quest for an ancient stash of Austrian gold galleons, the central concern of the text would be napkins, with each character contemplating just what a napkin means to both them and the world at large. For Galván, ample in his minorness, a napkin is simply a thoughtless means of tidying up his face and person after a meal of any size. More original and idiosyncratic in scope, for Yana a napkin is something to study rather than use. The napkins provided by the host or restaurant, of course, tell far more about the nature of the attendant design (aesthetics; utility) than the actual food might ever hope to. She parses this assertion endlessly, chapter by chapter, from linen squares to cheap paper cocktails. It's the hierarchical that Felicity, the novel's central character, is most interested in. Working in Acquisitions in the Slavic Studies Department at an Ivy League university, she regularly travels to Eastern Europe. There she makes note of what she doesn't see—namely, napkins. Although the places she visits are often far cleaner than anywhere in North America and, even in the midst of the intermittent societal upheaval and cultural transformation, the citizens of those places are more spotless and kempt than any others she has witnessed the whole world over, Felicity rarely if ever spies a cloth or paper napkin (recycled or otherwise) to accompany all this order. Meals are deliberate, rushed or ornately involved—and cleanly consumed no matter which. Becoming obsessed, Felicity searches and searches, her lack of progress somehow confirming her hypothesis that napkins are to slovenliness as oxygen is to air; expectation begets actuality.

One day Felicity wakes up and studies the heretofore ignored crumbs on the edge of her lonely hotel writing desk and, aged just 44, collapses dead from exhaustion, vintage terra cotta napkin ring in one hand, pristine four ply dinner napkin in the other. It is at this point that the novel would, stridently and imperceptibly, begin to cohere into a künstlerroman of a kind, albeit one that refuses the satisfaction of an earned maturity. The years pass unevenly in dreams, ¼ flying, ¼ drowning. After eating my schnitzel I wipe my face on my lapel, first the right, then the left. Ceaselessly I reload the pencil in my head, clear off the tablet in my mind. Intoxicated by a future. ¼ landlocked, ¼ tongue-tied. ¼ besought by the research of wonder. I could see it all so clearly, the way she would walk into a room fingers first, searching; her innocuous jacket, shoes, socks. Once.

Your X-Rays Have Just Come Back from the Lab and We Think We Know What Your Problem Is

Indigent, shimmering, the pieces of reality that I like best are the ones that fit together so finely—minutes rubbing into hours unto days funneling themselves (aghast!) into years—that it feels like your whole life is a déjà vu, pervasive, splatters of consciousness at every edge and the accretion shards of sight and motion and sound, lived out whole.

Nothing of the Month Club
"I have no friends, and you're one of them."
—Agnes Martin

Nothing of the Month Club

Later, at the lodge, we drank sun tea out of red plastic cups, watched the snowflakes steadily bloom into raindrops.

To our left Jake was actualizing for us the 7 rules of magic— *Exploit pattern recognition/Make the secret a lot more trouble than the trick seems worth/It's hard to think critically if you're laughing/ Keep the trickery outside of the frame/ To fool the mind, combine at least two tricks/ Nothing fools you better than the lie you tell yourself/ If you are given a choice, you believe you have acted freely—* and, bored with his soliloquy, no one cared to notice when by the end of it he'd lit a cigarette without using his hands.

"Flowers are colorful. And pretty," Shelia said, her bangs relentlessly flirting with her unibrow. "Especially the kind of flowers that grow out of cracks in the sidewalk. They remind me that every thing sometimes feels how I once felt."

To our right, Lloyd was reciting his new mantra under his breath, repeatingly: *...tomorrow I have the life I've always wanted it's called tomorrow I have the life I've always wanted it's called tomorrow I have the life I've always wanted it's called tomorrow I have the life I've always wanted it's called tomorrow I have—*

His fly was artfully undone, the knuckles on his clenched fists the size of performance-enhanced peanuts. Outside the raindrops steadily bloomed into clouds, clouds into orange and red cracks fissuring a darkening sky. We were suddenly out of sun tea, simply stuck with ourselves. Time, it seems, explains nothing about itself. Tomorrow I have—

Nothing of the Month Club

Summer. We switched the colors in our town's only traffic light to blue, pink and purple. Lo-card country-grade acid. A sun-soaked caramel apple, festering, steady the hour settles on my coffin's cover. Loving freely and boring easily, I changed my phone number to CALIFORNIA. (The stupid screen's still cracked, the screen's always cracked.) Death is the one and only law with no flaw. Dust into dust. Don't call me. Don't text.

Nothing of the Month Club

Owner of the world's largest air guitar collection, its loudest silence, a tender god is a tender god is a yielding gift to oneself, but don't quit your day job early, waiting for a fix. Wish. Out of boredom I throw all these dumb clumps of beauty into the river. They sink right quick. Rain, sun, sleet, snow, silence: It's not even noon and already today five different types of weather. Scampi's prepared hot and rich and rich. Huh?

The scrap metal that I planted by the reservoir last spring is finally starting to bloom!

A thousand white winter weddings soon upon us!

Nothing of the Month Club

Look me in the eyes when you stab me in the back the woman thought to herself, slamming back a 32-oz. bottle of Pepto-Bismol, naked, absently staring at herself in the bathroom's fluorescently lit full-length mirror, her bloated stomach a pot of fool's gold, barren, pregnant with guel and bile. Belly button the size of a silver dollar. She felt fine she felt fine she felt fine.

*

The woman typed *how to fold a burrito so the filling doesn't fall out* into the invisible engine filled with quantifiable numerical codes analytically transformed into linguistically readable searches and *how to fold a burrito so the feeling doesn't fall out* appeared on the screen instead. She scrutinized her finding, decided burritos were none of her business. Outside the library's computer lab the world was filled with shapes and colors constantly rising and falling in size, stature. The expression on the woman's face might best be described as glowful. She still needed to go to the market. She needed to make salsa.

Nothing of the Month Club

Most German fairy tales end with the sentence "Not long afterwards, there was an outbreak of the plague," and so the sudden death of a thousand fictional schoolchildren living in the Maxvorstadt proves imagination is a fact, fact with a spurious relationship to the truth. Hey Mr. Police Officer, if you're so smart how come you're only doing your job? Hey Mr. President, if you're so smart how come you're only doing your job? Hey Mr. Prime Minister, if you're so smart how come—. Did you know that in Mexico you have to *pay* to go to high school? Dumb American kids like myself are f-u-c-k-i-n-g lazy. Yesterday I studied the sky for hours, coming away with the realization that I can do nothing I am not against the emotional smear campaign otherwise known as life. I'm too smart. Horizon, cloud, the sky was crowded yesterday. I will mention the dead birds. I will mention the heavy wind. Will mention that what the wind makes out of the air is a bird's burden, wings ceaselessly swimming sky. "Oh a stately pleasure-dome decree/ Where Alph, the sacred river, ran/ Through caverns measureless to man/Down to a sunless sea." Flying is for the birds. Where eagles dare. I ain't no god-damned son of a bitch. Death exists at the border of fact and imagination and some fatal acceptance seals it. Hey Mr. Policeman, if you're so smart—. And so ends the tale of little boy Gunther and Stalvirt, the magical horse that saved all of Munich. Not long afterwards, there was an outbreak of the plague.

Nothing of the Month Club

Speech's surf is wavy, water's rift moodshopping a Babel more oblong than unintelligible. The rain before the sun and the darkness before the moon. Looking for any, only finding some, this train is made of colorless swathes and swatches, deaf each passenger's stammerings and—

                      great gout of self and loneliness—

alive, alive.

Nothing of the Month Club

Studying the bones in a blade of grass, squirms in a cube of ice, I've finally begun the major work necessary to finish my novella *I'm a Man of Few Words, None of Them About Myself.* I've resigned myself to the cold storage world of America, everhard. I've committed myself to a constant erection of the heart, evertaut.

Living in the moment before dying into the past, living in the moment before dying into the past, living in the moments.

Nothing of the Month Club

Certainly I've torn starlings apart with my bare hands, while smoking a cigar watched a pack of ravenous wasps methodically inhale a horse's head until only remained that glorious desecration. Color always wins. Color wins always. Color always wins but some blood lasts long past midnight's red.

Clockwork, when I was an abortionist I used to whiten my teeth every 3rd Thursday of the month. In the summer when it's bright out, flesh flowering everywhere, I miss that job. O what isn't an endless act of fore-suffered pre-destination? The sun flaws against the evergreen grove beside me this afternoon like some piteous act of charity and suddenly I'm fussy. Surely my mother loved me too much or never enough.

Get back.

How matters
more than

what.

Nothing of the Month Club

Honey hones its honesty right off the comb, no distillation needed. What is sweet in Athens is sweet in Oakland, in Ames. At the party last night I drank until I drowned. This morning my body language spoke only in spasms and stutters, the twelve months of my face clouded with rain. Contagious, cavities are _____. Bee stings fucking bite. If beauty is truth, truth beauty, remember to always bring a spoon. Consider portion-control.

Nothing of the Month Club

What I want is a tall thin husband that hogs the ball, has always, will always. Not to study Spanish over a prolonged period of time but to suddenly speak Spanish fluently, *sin esfuerzo*. A complete fasting of the mind, the moss and thick underbrush covering its outer shell worn in the manner of a redheaded woman wearing her curly red hair. *Me entiendes*? A bright spring day suddenly rinsing out this ash of enveloping smog the world entire. What I want is a tall man with a thin face peering with great intent into a thick book. But a coloring book! Surely my husband will not be able to read! *Como nativo sería hablarlo.* Bones of steel encased in fluffy white clouds. H2O mixed with CO2. Permanent fasting of the mind.

Nothing of the Month Club

Yesterday stands all over today facefucking tomorrow—I don't know. Америка-это как раз всё время is the shit my supplier says every time I pay him in cash. Мой дом-ваш дом, дорогой друг, но вы не срёте, где я сплю, не правда ли? It's the questions that don't start that won't stop. Will the stream run a long distance from the word *compliant* to the word *revolution*, the word *nononononononononono*? Power isn't. I can't un

Nothing of the Month Club

Today you're a lukewarm bubble bath while eating a cold caramel sundae while live tweeting the 1973 Academy Awards telecast, the one where Brando won Best Actor for *The Godfather* but declined both the award and the invitation to show up at the ceremony, Sacheen Littlefeather instead appearing in his place. After refusing to take the statuette from Roger Moore she implores the audience that only when the film industry's treatment of Native Americans is changed will Marlon be able to accept his Best Actor Oscar; only when "our hearts and our understandings are met with love and generosity." Seeing this you tweet three ☹ ☹ ☹, followed by the mysterious admission, "Life is too short & art is too long." Your 694 followers understand the point all too well. "The Beatles are bigger than Jesus," you say out loud to the dissipating bubbles. "But would you let your daughter marry a Rolling Stone?" Suddenly, slowly, the bathwater is so tepid you can smell your heart, its soggy ventricles, moldy recesses. Black shampoo, black shampoo. "I'm more fucked up than a soup sandwich," you plead to the bathroom walls. "More fucked than a sandwich made solely of slippery soup."

Nothing of the Month Club

Tonight let the finish line slide beneath me of its own accord and let the sky's panoply, dumb with stars, cease its brilliant winter. Tonight the Soup of the Day at my favorite restaurant is tequila and, so very hungry, I'm 14 minutes sober—what to do, what to do? Tomorrow will be another morning—let's call it a life—spent searching the medicine cabinet for aspirin and finding instead cheeseburger wrappers, half-smoked cigars. And the future a dream I had last night, one I'll never remember. There's a sickness in me, I'm sure. From a mile away you can hear me smile. A sickness.

Resignation Modes

My dog won't stop jumping on the couch, so eventually I love him for it. My husband can't keep a steady job, so instead I grow inordinately fond of his ambient sound collages. Since he will not, I eventually try to sell them on his behalf. If to love is to be resigned to compromise, the compromiser and the compromisé soon forget who is who, which renegotiation is being renegotiated unto what agreement that needs to be thought through anew.

*

Full of faith, the priest accepts his parishioners' petty deceits and deceptions in the manner of a man lowering his head at a low doorway, ducking down slowly, incrementally, then after passing through rising up straight again, straighter even than before.

*

The best lies are the ones that eventually turn true.

*

The plumber peers under the sink knowing that every clog in the drain masks a larger problem, one that he will never be able to fix. Knowledge of this fact keeps him going. It proves his self is different than his worth. Serenely, it enables him to succeed.

*

At the end of a long day, each thought the name of a beautiful city in a foreign country that you can't properly pronounce. You can't stop thinking them.

*

Later, I ask someone twenty years older than me: *Do you remember when you first began attending to your desires with muted inattention? Not with despair but indifference; not with sorrow but detachment, unroiled and inert?* She responds a month later, months after I'd given up on receiving a response:

If at your age you're already thinking about that, you've crossed the threshold. Welcome home—oblivion is free!

*

In private, only to herself, the great writer resigns herself to her greatness immediately and such an internal resolution never wavers. By the literary community, too, she is quickly accepted and praised as great; what idiosyncratic vision, what fluidity of voice. She performs such greatness with aplomb, accepting every honor and award humbly, taking care to insist on her relative mediocrity, the superior craftsmanship of her many lesser-known friends. For this she is even more beloved, widely read by the critics and public alike. It is only on her deathbed that she realizes the full extent of the thing, unwavering and remarkable. Then, awake for the first time, the possibility comes into her head that she might never have been great.

*

"Fu Yüeh was once in bonds, before he was minister to Wu-ting. So, disaster is to fortune as strands to a single rope."

"Let your life be like a floating, your death like a rest."

"Find no cause for complacency in life, but cultivate emptiness and drift…Be not dismayed by petty pricks and checks!"

Perhaps the Taoists understand best that happiness is rarely earned or understood; it exists with scant relation to work or virtue, knowledge or ignorance. That's what makes it attainable to any and everyone. That's what makes it impossible and free.

*

But I don't want to be a genius! the young genius laments to anyone in earshot. The petulance, the outbursts, the heavy sighs, the outbursts. As prodigy exhausts, prophecy invokes: the busy parents in the background, from one practice to another rushing to-and-fro, their prodigies simultaneously eager and withdrawn. *I just want to be me* he sobs into his pillow. *I just want to be me* she screams before slamming the door.

*

Reporting on the city's homeless population, the newscaster interviews a man who unblinkingly repeats into the camera the sentence *Those that live this life to steal, come back to be stolen from.* Over and over again, until finally he has to be gently pulled away by an idle videographer. The producers later decide that what the camera captures of the man the audience should not see, and the footage is cut in the editing room. But the newscaster never forgets the man's words. Having tried and failed not to listen, she unconsciously resigns herself to a theft that all the reporting in the world will never be able to accurately cover. What has she stolen? She herself doesn't know, but it's a lingering that refuses to subside, that must have purchase by virtue of its lifelong prolongment in her head. After that night, she never sees the man again, even forgets him and his prophecy during the happier times of her life, but inevitably she drifts back to the righteousness of his conclusion. Lacking God and a belief in reincarnation, she accepts his proclamation as something she cannot understand and has no power to refute. Loyalty of the deepest kind, it haunts her unreservedly.

*

Define best.

*

Владивостока.   Σμύρνη.   Huánucovenird.

*

At the start of his career the politician resigns himself to the fact that progress is a great ship that only incrementally makes headway through the vast and turbulent waters. This lack soothes him, enforces the notion that he is a mere cog in a machine, that nothing is much expected of him other than his ability to get re-elected. Surprising himself most of all, by the end of his career he has done so much good for so many people. Still, he believes in little— not bureaucracy nor democracy, not politics. Fingers interlocked, not a pair of hands held too tightly together; not humanity. For a very short period of time he is a mere deckhand on that ship, destination unknown. At every reelection party, he raises his arms in victory, pure, hollow.

*

What the arsonist doesn't understand about herself she incinerates. But in the chars left behind are modes of thought and dream still more mysterious.

*

The worst lies are those that fester into a firm handshake looking you right in the eye, dead center, the way they smile showing all their teeth, straight, white, precise.

*

The painter lives his life in revolt of the six primary colors he has been given. He does not desire more, but he does envision another realm of possibility, where light and dark are not opposites that attract, deadended, but instead are pressure points that ascertain how something as constant as oxygen can be as colorless as air. Choose your essentiality but make sure you choose the right one, the essential one. Just words, I know. But in his work the painter takes care to make each hue sound like a slipping, smell like *over there, over there, it happened right over there.* Violet, blue, green, yellow, orange, red.

*

A jugular nerve, a sunspotted moon-pock only visible with a powerful telescope, the actress assesses her career at the age of sixty. Height of her power, all's slowing down, roles sparse or middling. At twenty-five she'd attached herself to her ambition with a feral clarity. Now her enmity is silent and precise, devoid of any mitigating assurance or sense of redemption. When you look into that telescope what you see is far from hidden—then and now it is visible, it shines.

*

Swaying in the wind or stewing in the rain, each blade of grass resigns itself to a green it will never be.

*

The priest ducks his head at the low doorway, rises straight once again. The priest ducks his head at the low doorway, rises straight once again. The priest ducks his head at the low doorway, rises straight once again.

*

We hope to resign ourselves to hope. It sometimes feels impossible to get there. Knowing that it won't be taken out, the dog won't stop whining to go out.

*

I want to be me. Over and over in petite voices, virulent in their stridency. *I want to be me.* Just ignore them and they'll go away, grow up to be glorious or themselves. *I want, I want.* They'll see.

The Natural Way To Draw

We were learning how to draw properly, the way an actual artist would. Our teacher read aloud from the handout she'd passed out at the beginning of class, the one with no pictures:

Contour and Line: *We think of the figure composed of the apparent lines around the structural forms of the body. Of course, there are no actual lines on the figure unless you take a piece of crayon and draw some on it. The edge of the figure, which you may heretofore have thought of as a line, is in reality simply the place where the figure ceases to exist. Whenever you think of lines and whenever you use them in drawing, you should realize that the figure is inside your lines and that actually there are no lines on the figure. LINES, IF YOU THINK OF THEM AT ALL, ARE CAUSED BY THE FIGURE. They are not separate from the figure but a part of it.*

She kept going, the air conditioner's guttural heartstrings repeatedly murmuring their assent. Out the window the lone teeter-totter on the deserted playground swung wildly up and down, from a distance its movement appearing as neither accident nor omen. It was almost summertime and cloudless. No wind. The monkey-bars veritably glistened. On the deserted playground the teeter-totter swung back and forth, up and down, back and forth in the stillborn heat…

The Puppy Still Hasn't Opened Her Eyes

In New York it was in Berlin. In Berlin it was in Tokyo. In Tokyo it was in Amsterdam. In Amsterdam it was in Melbourne. In Melbourne in Prague, in Prague in Marfa, in Marfa in Mendocino, in Mendocino in New York. Quicksand's solidity, our restlessness was determined only by our ability to identify a future that derived from our inaccurate understanding of the past. (The granite colonnades we're leaning against are slathered with mud and encased in Jell-O, swaying in the spring breeze.) Despair is believing tomorrow will be exactly the same as today, which was exactly the same as yesterday, which was no more than a bird call heard precise and clear above the city street, then left unanswered in the midst of rush hour. In Guadalajara our therapists had prescribed an early bedtime and a gratitude journal; in Victoria they had advocated for finding our "social genius" within the maelstrom, taking the time to stay up late, celebrate. One has to figure out who they don't want to be in Durango by being that unwanted person in Ashland and so in Vienna we interstice, arms outstretched at our sides, fingernails clipped, shirts pressed but left untucked. (The granite colonnades we're pressing hard against are shaking with the vibrations of the winter squall, moisture of another summer tempest.)

Monkey Puzzle Roots

Solitude is earned in a thousand messages in a bottle thrown into the ocean and none answered. Or how with age pleasure becomes a responsibility, not a privilege. Same *Make Your Orgasm Deeper— and Longer Lasting!* magazine hovering at the checkout stand your entire life. Same regressive dinner parties, validating the flood of companied confusion. Love's emotional trigonometry. Time. Doubt.

Last Exit

Soon after his birth the son and mother were separated, and when reunited 19 years later she spoke only English and he only Turkish. The conversation stilted in the way an overwatered plant initially stands resolute with sustenance, then swiftly topples.

"You've certainly made it all the way through!" she said to him in English. "Mother! Mother! I can hardly see your face, I am so overcome," he said to her in Turkish. She thanked him; he apologized. Then a silence, both too long and too short. Each swallowed the murmur of a dead end in their mouths but refused to acknowledge it. The mother ruffled the son's hair, then stopped when he burrowed into her touch.

Stray
    after Ray Johnson

Then I saw a blind woman
in the supermarket
checkout line
with about forty items
in a ten-items-or-less line.
She was maybe 65 years old.
There were a lot of people
lined up
behind her.
6 by my count.
This was at 6:20 PM
on a Wednesday in July,
arguably peak supermarket
shopping time.
I believe that lofty pronouncements
and declarations
are things to disparage
in life, in art
and literature. Mostly.
Like the stray dog
that my neighbor Jim feeds
when he wants to
and doesn't
when he doesn't.
Jim's divorced, in the insurance business,
and I think he owns his apartment
outright. But I have no
real sense of these things
beyond the unwarranted
airs of superiority
that manifest themselves
in cologne onslaughts, bulbous
wrists filled
with too much calcium.
I don't know
dogs, though, not really,
at least not

in the way
that, say,
I know
what it's like to miss
the last 19 bus
on the S Line
and have to hoof it
home on foot,
the darkness a kind of performance
art piece, ascending
while descending.
It doesn't have a name,
the stray. Or maybe
it does, intuits what
to respond to
depending on the offer and situation.
Jim calls it
Here Little Guy,
Here You Go,
There You Go,
All Of It,
Whoa,
Don't Go
Too Fast Now,
There You Go,
That's Alright, There
You Go.
Now. That
Was. There
You Go.
Or doesn't.
That July was so hot,
especially that night.
I could hardly work
on my square breathing, deep
breaths, peaceful thoughts.
The blind woman
took her items out
one by one,
slowly and carefully,
and no one helped
and no one said

anything.
Some shift manager
didn't materialize
to assuage everyone's feelings
and let us leave
or forget.
Stuck, we
just watched.
Bright
fluorescent lights.

Notes

Nothing of the Month Club takes its title from a phrase used in a collage by the artist Ray Johnson.

The Ai Weiwei epigraph in "The Leopard Does Not Change Its Spots" is from Sarah Thornton's *33 Artists in 3 Acts* (Norton).

"Your X-Rays Have Just Come Back from the Lab and We Think We Know What Your Problem Is" takes its title from the Jets to Brazil song of the same name.

The Agnes Martin epigraph in the "Nothing of the Month Club" section is from Nancy Princenthal's *Agnes Martin: Her Life and Art* (Thames & Hudson).

Many of the poems in this collection were inspired by the work of the Russian OBERIU group, namely Alexander Vvedensky, Nikolay Zabolotsky and Daniil Kharms. Edited by Eugene Ostashevsky, the volume *OBERIU: An Anthology of Russian Absurdism* (Northwestern University Press) has been extremely important to me. I previously wrote a bit about my connection to the OBERIU group at the Poetry Society of America website:

https://poetrysociety.org/features/in-their-own-words/jeff-alessandrelli-on-be-yer-own-hitman-deathsounds-lovesongs

---

Acknowledgements

Some of these poems originally appeared at *A Dozen Nothing, Propeller, Witness, Burnside Review, Map Literary, Gold Wake Online* and *Old Pal*. "The problem of America is my body" was included in the anthology *Bodyprint: An Anthology of the Body*, edited by Justin Rigamonti.

"Resignation Modes" and most of the "Nothing of the Month Club" poems were originally published in the collection *Fur Not Light* (Burnside Review Press, 2019). Thank you to the editors.

Thanks to Aaron Kent and everyone at *Broken Sleep*.
Thanks to Justin Rigamonti, for his help, advice and support.
Thanks to *Burnside Review Press*, which published *Fur Not Light*.

Thank you.

LAY OUT YOUR UNREST